Current
CONTROVERSIES

Death Penalty

DISCARD

Other Books in the Current Controversies Series

Death Penalty

Noël Merino, Book Editor

GREENHAVEN PRESS
A part of Gale, Cengage Learning

GALE
CENGAGE Learning·

Farmington Hills, Mich • San Francisco • New York • Waterville, Maine
Meriden, Conn • Mason, Ohio • Chicago

Patricia Coryell, *Vice President & Publisher, New Products & GVRL*
Douglas Dentino, *Manager, New Products*
Judy Galens, *Acquisitions Editor*

Articles in Greenhaven Press anthologies are often edited for length to meet page requirements. In addition, original titles of these works are changed to clearly present the main thesis and to explicitly indicate the author's opinion. Every effort is made to ensure that Greenhaven Press accurately reflects the original intent of the authors. Every effort has been made to trace the owners of copyrighted material.

Cover image copyright © Scott Olson/Hulton Archive/Getty Images.

LIBRARY OF CONGRESS CATALOGING-IN-PUBLICATION DATA

Death penalty / Noël Merino, book editor.
   pages cm. -- (Current controversies)
   Includes bibliographical references and index.
   ISBN 978-0-7377-7213-5 (hardcover) -- ISBN 978-0-7377-7214-2 (pbk.)
   1. Capital punishment--United States. I. Merino, Noël.
   HV8699.U5D3562 2015
   364.660973--dc23
                                                  2014039597

Printed in the United States of America
1 2 3 4 5   19 18 17 16 15

Contents

Chapter 1: Is the Death Penalty Just and Ethical?

Chapter 3: Is the Death Penalty Applied Fairly?

Most prisoners with death sentences are male and just over half are white, and many end up with their sentence commuted or overturned. Of the more than eight thousand inmates sentenced to death from 1977 to 2012, only 16 percent were eventually executed.

Yes: The Death Penalty Is Applied Fairly

No: The Death Penalty Is Not Applied Fairly

Chapter 4: How Should US Death Penalty Practices Be Reformed?

In cases of convicted murderers of horrible crimes and where guilt is certain, there is no good argument against the death penalty. Cherry-picking questionable death-row cases to underscore the fallibility of capital punishment, as opponents of the system typically do, does not render the death penalty unjust or unwarranted for those murderers whose guilt is beyond any doubt.

Foreword

By definition, controversies are "discussions of questions in which opposing opinions clash" (Webster's Twentieth Century Dictionary Unabridged). Few would deny that controversies are a pervasive part of the human condition and exist on virtually every level of human enterprise. Controversies transpire between individuals and among groups, within nations and between nations. Controversies supply the grist necessary for progress by providing challenges and challengers to the status quo. They also create atmospheres where strife and warfare can flourish. A world without controversies would be a peaceful world; but it also would be, by and large, static and prosaic.

The Series' Purpose

The purpose of the Current Controversies series is to explore many of the social, political, and economic controversies dominating the national and international scenes today. Titles selected for inclusion in the series are highly focused and specific. For example, from the larger category of criminal justice, Current Controversies deals with specific topics such as police brutality, gun control, white collar crime, and others. The debates in Current Controversies also are presented in a useful, timeless fashion. Articles and book excerpts included in each title are selected if they contribute valuable, long-range ideas to the overall debate. And wherever possible, current information is enhanced with historical documents and other relevant materials. Thus, while individual titles are current in focus, every effort is made to ensure that they will not become quickly outdated. Books in the Current Controversies series will remain important resources for librarians, teachers, and students for many years.

In addition to keeping the titles focused and specific, great care is taken in the editorial format of each book in the series. Book introductions and chapter prefaces are offered to provide background material for readers. Chapters are organized around several key questions that are answered with diverse opinions representing all points on the political spectrum. Materials in each chapter include opinions in which authors clearly disagree as well as alternative opinions in which authors may agree on a broader issue but disagree on the possible solutions. In this way, the content of each volume in Current Controversies mirrors the mosaic of opinions encountered in society. Readers will quickly realize that there are many viable answers to these complex issues. By questioning each author's conclusions, students and casual readers can begin to develop the critical thinking skills so important to evaluating opinionated material.

Current Controversies is also ideal for controlled research. Each anthology in the series is composed of primary sources taken from a wide gamut of informational categories including periodicals, newspapers, books, US and foreign government documents, and the publications of private and public organizations. Readers will find factual support for reports, debates, and research papers covering all areas of important issues. In addition, an annotated table of contents, an index, a book and periodical bibliography, and a list of organizations to contact are included in each book to expedite further research.

Perhaps more than ever before in history, people are confronted with diverse and contradictory information. During the Persian Gulf War, for example, the public was not only treated to minute-to-minute coverage of the war, it was also inundated with critiques of the coverage and countless analyses of the factors motivating US involvement. Being able to sort through the plethora of opinions accompanying today's major issues, and to draw one's own conclusions, can be a complicated and frustrating struggle. It is the editors' hope that Current Controversies will help readers with this struggle.

Introduction

> "*Although the US Supreme Court has never interpreted the Eighth Amendment's prohibition on cruel and unusual punishment to completely prevent the states from administering the death penalty, it has placed constitutional limits on the practice.*"

The death penalty, or capital punishment, has existed as a punishment for centuries in countries throughout the world. In the United States, the death penalty has been practiced since the founding of the country, although—as today—it has always varied by state. Since criminal sanctions are administered by the states (except in the case of federal crimes), each state determines its own policy with respect to punishment, including whether or not it allows capital punishment and, if so, for which crimes. However, the US Constitution places limits on the criminal justice practices of the states through the Eighth Amendment, which demands, "Excessive bail shall not be required, nor excessive fines imposed, nor cruel and unusual punishments inflicted." Although the US Supreme Court has never interpreted the Eighth Amendment's prohibition on cruel and unusual punishment to completely prevent the states from administering the death penalty, it has placed constitutional limits on the practice.

In 1972, the US Supreme Court, in a group of cases known collectively as *Furman v. Georgia*, determined that when the death sentence is given in a way that is arbitrary or capricious it is in violation of the Eighth Amendment. The Court reasoned that a punishment is "cruel and unusual" if the people who receive it are, as Justice Potter Stewart put it, "among a capriciously selected random handful upon whom the sentence of death has in fact been imposed." The justices expressed a variety of concerns about the way the states were administering the death penalty, including concerns that it was administered in a way that suggested racial bias. The result of the opinion was a nationwide moratorium on the death penalty while states looked at ways to avoid the unconstitutional arbitrariness identified by the Court.

Several states attempted to eliminate arbitrary discretion by juries and judges by providing sentencing guidelines for determining whether to impose the death penalty that allowed for aggravating and mitigating factors. The Supreme Court approved the revised death penalty statutes of Georgia, Florida, and Texas in 1976 in a collective case known as *Gregg v. Georgia*, noting that the death penalty itself was constitutional under the Eighth Amendment:

> Considerations of federalism, as well as respect for the ability of a legislature to evaluate, in terms of its particular State, the moral consensus concerning the death penalty and its social utility as a sanction, require us to conclude, in the absence of more convincing evidence, that the infliction of death as a punishment for murder is not without justification, and thus is not unconstitutionally severe.

The Court determined that if the sentence of death is given according to objective criteria and if the particular character of the defendant can be taken into account, the death penalty is allowed under the US Constitution.

Since the Court's decision in *Gregg*, it has placed other constitutional limits on the use of the death penalty. The Court has determined that the death penalty may not be given for the crime of rape when the victim does not die, reasoning that to do so would constitute a disproportionate punishment, in violation of the Eighth Amendment. The Court has also ruled that it is unconstitutional to give minors under the age of eighteen and the mentally handicapped a sentence of death, determining that such a punishment would be cruel and unusual and, thus, constitutionally forbidden.

Although the Supreme Court has allowed that the states have discretion in allowing capital punishment, not all states permit the death penalty. As of August 2014, thirty-two states have the death penalty and eighteen states do not. Six of the states that have banned the death penalty did so since 2007, illustrating a trend in the United States away from capital punishment. That said, a majority of Americans still support the death penalty and a majority of the states still offer death as a mode of punishment. The current debates about the death penalty in the United States are explored in *Current Controversies: Death Penalty*, illustrating the opposing viewpoints that are taken on this complicated issue.

CHAPTER 1

Is the Death Penalty Just and Ethical?

Overview: View of Death Penalty as Morally OK Unchanged in US

Jeffrey M. Jones

Jeffrey M. Jones is managing editor of the Gallup Poll.

The recent news about the botched execution of an Oklahoma death row inmate has not affected the way Americans view the death penalty. Sixty-one percent say the death penalty is morally acceptable, similar to the 62% who said so in 2013, although both figures are down from a high of 71% in 2006.

The results are based on Gallup's annual Values and Beliefs poll, conducted May 8–11. On April 29, an Oklahoma death row inmate given a lethal injection appeared to suffer for an extended period of time until finally dying of a heart attack. That incident led to the postponement of a second execution scheduled in Oklahoma that day and raised questions about the methods used to execute prisoners.

The case did not fundamentally alter Americans' perceptions of the death penalty, however, with a solid majority viewing it as morally acceptable. This percentage is similar to the 60% who say they favor the death penalty as punishment for murder in Gallup's October update.

But the longer-term trends reveal that Americans have become less supportive of the death penalty. Gallup first asked the moral acceptability question in 2001, with an average 66% saying it was acceptable between 2001 and the peak in 2006. Over the last three years, the percentage saying it is morally acceptable has averaged 60%.

Similarly, Americans' support for the death penalty as a punishment for murder is also trending downward. Support reached a high of 80% in 1994, but it has generally slipped since then.

Americans Still Say Lethal Injection Most Humane Form of Execution

Lethal injection has been the most common method state officials have used to execute death row inmates for many years. The American public generally approves of that approach, as the poll finds Americans overwhelmingly saying lethal injection is the most humane way to administer the death penalty. The 65% holding this view compares with between 4% and 9% who endorse another method—the electric chair, gas chamber, firing squad, or hanging—as the most humane way to execute someone sentenced to death.

Americans have long supported the death penalty, with majorities saying they favor it as a penalty for murder and believe it is morally acceptable.

Gallup has asked this question twice before, and although 23 years have elapsed since the question was last asked, the results today have changed little. In 1991, 67% said lethal injection was the most humane method for administering the death penalty, and in 1985, 56% said this.

A majority of those who view the death penalty as morally acceptable and those who view it as morally wrong say lethal injection is the most humane way to execute prisoners. However, this belief is more common among those who say the death penalty is acceptable. Notably, roughly one in four of those who say the death penalty is morally wrong volunteer that "no method" is the most humane way to execute someone.

Implications

The drawn-out death of the Oklahoma prisoner reignited the debate over whether the death penalty violates the Constitution's prohibition of "cruel and unusual" punishment. The U.S. Supreme Court invalidated state death penalty statutes in the 1972 case *Furman v. Georgia*, deciding that death sentences were often arbitrary and consequently were a form of cruel and unusual punishment. Later, in the 1976 *Gregg v. Georgia* judgment, the Supreme Court ruled that states' rewritten statutes did pass constitutional muster, leading to a resumption of the death penalty in the U.S.

Americans have long supported the death penalty, with majorities saying they favor it as a penalty for murder and believe it is morally acceptable. While both of these Gallup trends show diminished support for the death penalty in recent years, the trends were in place well before the Oklahoma case.

Q&A: Death Penalty Proponent Robert Blecker

Robert Blecker, interviewed by Rodger Jones

Robert Blecker is professor of law at New York Law School. He is interviewed by Dallas News *editorial writer Rodger Jones.*

Our Q&A is with New York Law School professor Robert Blecker, death penalty proponent and author. Based on thousands of hours inside maximum security prisons and on death rows in several states, his recently published crime-and-punishment memoir *The Death of Punishment* urges a fresh look at our criminal justice system.

You have heard the arguments from appellate lawyers who are trying to block executions that use untried drugs, based on the objection they might cause pain. What's your reaction?

This whole controversy obscures deeper disagreements about the death penalty itself. Abolitionists—those who oppose capital punishment—try to clog the system with specious attacks. Clearly we can administer a lethal anesthetic to painlessly kill. Why should the FDA approve the drug? This is not medicine to cure; it's poison to kill.

A massive dose of anesthetic might produce dying twitches, making it falsely appear that the condemned, completely unconscious, experiences pain. To maximize its deterrent effect, ideally punishment should *appear* painful to the public while actually experienced as painless to the punished.

I once witnessed an execution. It struck me as obscenely similar to my father-in-law's death in a hospice: The dying lay on a gurney, wrapped in white sheets, an IV in his arm, poison coursing through his veins.

How we kill those we love should never resemble how we kill those we rightly detest. Thus, I too, oppose lethal injection, not because it possibly causes pain, but because it certainly causes confusion—conflating medicine with punishment.

What form of execution do you favor?

I prefer the firing squad. I would allow a representative of the victim's family, if they wanted, to take the first shot from any range, before the sharpshooters finished the execution.

In your book, you lay out the case for retributive justice, kind of a just-deserts doctrine. Please explain.

We have the responsibility to punish those who deserve it, but only to the degree they deserve it. Retributivists do not justify the death penalty by the general deterrence or safety it brings us. And we reject over-punishing no less than under-punishing. How obscene that aggravated murderers who behave well inside prison watch movies and play softball.

We must never allow our satisfaction at doing justice to deteriorate into sadistic revenge.

We also find it obscene, as the ACLU has recently documented, that 3,000 persons serve life without parole for non-violent crimes in the U.S. For all true retributivists, the past counts. Don't ask us what good will it do. Regardless of future benefits, we justify punishment because it's deserved. Let the punishment fit the crime. The past counts.

How does retribution differ from revenge, in your view?

Opponents wrongly equate retribution and revenge, because they both would inflict pain and suffering on those who have inflicted pain and suffering on us.

Whereas revenge knows no bounds, retribution must be limited, proportional and appropriately directed: The retributive punishment fits the crime. We must never allow our satisfaction at doing justice to deteriorate into sadistic revenge.

DNA tests have proven the fallibility of the U.S. justice system, something we've seen frequently in Texas. How do you defend capital punishment in light of that?

Social life proves the fallibility of every human institution. We do imperfectly define, detect, prosecute and punish crime. We have not yet provably but nevertheless have, most probably, executed an innocent person in the modern era. Any true retributivist feels sick at this thought. We support the mission of the Innocence Project.

Fortunately, as we raise the stakes we drastically reduce the mistakes. Before we sentence a defendant to life without parole, and especially before we condemn him to die, I would require a higher burden of persuasion than proof beyond a reasonable doubt. A jury should have no nagging doubts, however unreasonable. Before they sentence a person to die, a jury should be convinced beyond any residual doubt that he did it, and also be convinced "to a moral certainty" that he deserves to die.

Many times daily we risk the lives of those we love for the sake of convenience. Surely then, we will occasionally risk the lives of those we detest for the sake of justice.

You take issue with some death sentences, wondering whether the system has always targeted the "right people." Who are the "right people," and when has the system gone overboard?

We can never exactly and exhaustively define in advance the worst of the worst—those who most deserve to die. But thousands of hours documenting the lives and attitudes of convicted killers these past 25 years have shown me clear examples of who deserve to die.

As *The Death of Punishment* urges, we should reserve capital punishment for those who rape and murder, especially children or other vulnerable victims, serial killers, hired killers, torture killers, mass murderers, and terrorists.

It comes down to cruelty and viciousness, really: Did the killer exhibit intense pleasure or a selfish depraved, cold indifference? As Aristotle taught us, evil lies at the extremes.

As bizarre as this sounds, inside prisons it's nobody's job to punish.

At the same time, we should refine our death penalty statutes to eliminate other aggravating circumstances: Robbery-murder has put more killers on death row than any other aggravator, and too often unjustifiably so. Texas particularly makes a huge moral mistake, in my view, by focusing on future dangerousness, rather than past desert.

We can construct prisons to incapacitate the dangerous. We should only execute those who most deserve it. And not randomly. Refine our death penalty statutes and review the sentences of everyone on death row. Release into general population those who don't really deserve to die. The rest we should execute—worst first.

Overall, you suggest that the American system has lost its appetite for punishment. Can you explain?

As bizarre as this sounds, inside prisons it's nobody's job to punish. Consult the department of correction's mission statement in the 50 states, including Texas. You will not find the word "punishment."

Officers and prisoners in the many prisons I've visited in seven states—but not yet Texas—speak with one voice: "What a guy did out there is none of my business. I only care how he behaves once he's inside."

Vicious cowards who prey on the vulnerable, once captured, often become the best behaved—"good inmates" from corrections point of view. They live the good life inside prison, with the most privileges. Thus, even as we mouth it, we mock our basic credo of justice: Let the punishment fit the crime. Inside prison, too often, those who deserve it most, suffer least.

Explain your idea of "permanent punitive segregation" for convicted killers and how it is or isn't catching on among decision-makers.

Whether we keep or abolish death as punishment, we need to rethink prison for the worst of the worst. A jury should specially convict and condemn them to permanent punitive segregation. Life for them, every day, should be painful and unpleasant—the harshest conditions the Constitution allows.

They would eat only nutraloaf, a tasteless patty, nutritionally complete but offering no sensory pleasure. All visits should be non-contact and kept to a constitutional minimum. A person who rapes and murders a child, or tortures another to death should never touch another human being again.

These most heinous criminals would never watch TV. They would get one brief, lukewarm shower a week. Let photos of their victims adorn their cells—in their face but out of reach.

Connecticut, even as they abolished the death penalty, recently took steps in this direction. Let's reconnect crime with punishment. For the question of justice really is not whether they live or die, but how they live until they die.

Koch Death Penalty Arguments Still Persuasive

Jack Kenny

Jack Kenny writes for the New American.

The passing of former New York Mayor Ed Koch on February 1 brings to mind one of the most controversial things he ever did as a Democrat in the heart of American liberalism. In 1985, the three-term (January 1, 1978–December 31, 1989) mayor wrote an essay defending the death penalty. He even had the temerity to declare, "Life is indeed precious and I believe the death penalty helps to affirm that fact."

Though it outraged liberals and "progressives" among the nation's esteemed "intelligentsia," Koch's essay reflected the convictions of most Americans, then as now, as opinion polls have consistently shown a substantial majority in favor of the death penalty. Yet the issue has been hotly debated for decades, based on claims concerning the morality of a state-imposed sentence of death. In June 1972 the U.S. Supreme Court, in *Furman v. Georgia*, found the death penalty to be unconstitutional when sentences are handed down and executions are carried out in ways that are arbitrary or influenced by racial bias. The decision resulted in a de facto ban on executions nationwide, pending further word from the Court. They were resumed in 1976 under guidelines meant to provide greater consistency and eliminate racial discrimination in capital cases.

In broader terms, however, arguments have often centered on the issue of deterrence. Death penalty defenders have argued that the electric chair, the gas chamber, the hangman's noose, or lethal injection deterred people from killing others. Opponents argue the possibility of facing the death sentence has no deterrent effect on those who kill in crimes of passion or those who believe they won't get caught. One argument that defies refutation is that whomever else it may or may not deter, capital punishment surely deters the killer who has been caught, duly tried, and executed. That one will not kill again. Death penalty opponents argue, however, that we can achieve that goal just as well with sentences of life without parole.

Koch, writing at the time the electric chair was either still in use or within recent memory, cited the example of a man who boasted of being undeterred because the death penalty was not in force. "Consider the tragic death of Rosa Velez, who happened to be home when a man named Luis Vera burglarized her apartment in Brooklyn," Koch wrote. Vera admitted he shot and killed the woman. "She knew me, and I knew I wouldn't go to the chair," he later admitted.

Retribution is an essential component of justice and society, like individuals, has a right to self-defense against homicide.

Yet death penalty opponents would have us feel guilty as citizens when the state puts a killer to death for his crime or crimes. We are asked to believe that the state is hypocritical for punishing killing with killing. To recall a refrain from the 1960s, "Why do we kill people who kill people to show people that killing people is wrong?" One might say the same about a prison sentence for a kidnapper. Is the state wrong to imprison people for imprisoning people because imprisoning people is wrong? What should we do, short of treating every crime as a sickness that can be cured with shock therapy or some other form of "extreme makeover"?

Koch cited as a "curiosity of modern life" the spectacle of convicted murderers, when facing execution, lecturing the rest of society on the immorality of the death penalty. Such special pleading suggests the condemned killer is as much, if not more, sinned against than sinning. He may have killed someone in a fit of passion or desperate need for a quick financial gain. The state, on the other hand, will calmly and coolly throw the switch or inject the needle as a matter of simple retribution. An individual made a rash and foolish judgment. The state should know better.

But retribution is an essential component of justice and society, like individuals, has a right to self-defense against homicide. Again, death penalty abolitionists argue that a sentence of life without parole fulfills that need. Some death penalty defenders argue that the care and feeding of murderers until they die of old age in prison simply costs the state too much money. Opponents contend the legal costs of imposing the death penalty, after all the prisoner's appeals have been exhausted, outweighs the cost of imprisonment. Either argument is crass and hardly relevant in a debate over the sanctity of life and the demands of justice. Not everything can or should be determined by a cost-benefit analysis.

A problem with the life sentence alternative is that killers sometimes escape prison. Or they murder guards or other prisoners with impunity. Already sentenced to life, with the death penalty not available to the state, what do they have to lose? Then there is the question of proportionality. Are there not some crimes so heinous that the execution of the perpetrators is the only punishment that even remotely fits the crime?

The Bible has been argued over with more heat than light in the debate over the death penalty. "Thou shalt not kill" is undoubtedly one of the Ten Commandments, though it is clear the meaning in that context is "murder," or unlawful killing. Only committed pacifists believe killing an aggressor threatening one's own life or the life of another is inherently evil, or that killing soldiers of an invading army is murder.

And the law that came by Moses was not written for pacifists. God in the Old Testament frequently sent the Israelites off to war. And Exodus and Deuteronomy, where the Ten Commandments are found, prescribe the death penalty for a wide range of crimes. In Genesis, God is heard not only affirming the death penalty, but also offering a reason for it that anticipates Koch's argument; "Whosoever shall shed man's blood, his blood shall be shed: for man was made to the image of God" (Genesis 9:6).

If you were the parent of a six-year-old with a dozen bullet holes in his dead body, would you oppose a sentence of death for the child's killer?

Abolitionists often cite the New Testament story of the woman caught in adultery (John 8: 1–11) in an effort to enlist Jesus as a death penalty opponent. The law, the crowd pointed out, prescribed death by stoning for such an offense. (One shudders to think of the mortality rate if adultery were a capital crime in modern America.) But surely the fact that one might oppose a death sentence in some cases does not necessarily mean he would oppose it in all cases. Besides, even in those pre-Miranda times, the accused was entitled to some semblance of due process. And the gang that dragged the woman to Jesus appeared more like a lynch mob than a jury.

Koch in his essay offered the following simple and compelling argument: If we reduced the penalty for rape, he asked, would that show a greater or a lesser respect for women and human sexuality? The question really answers itself. So what does abolishing the death penalty say about our respect for life? "When we lower the penalty for murder," Koch wrote, "it signals a lessened regard for the value of the victim's life." The mayor also dismissed as "sophistic nonsense" the argument advanced by some death penalty opponents that a life sentence is actually a harsher punishment than the penalty of death. "A few killers may decide not to appeal a death sentence," he wrote, "but the overwhelming majority make every effort to stay alive."

Here is another question: Suppose the killer of the 20 first-graders and six faculty members at Sandy Hook School in Newtown, Connecticut, last December had not killed himself, but were sitting now in a jail cell awaiting trial. Suppose he were found legally sane. Would death penalty foes oppose the ultimate penalty for him? The question would be hypothetical even under those conditions, since Connecticut has abolished its death penalty. But if you were the parent of a six-year-old with a dozen bullet holes in his dead body, would you oppose a sentence of death for the child's killer?

No doubt some people would, holding fast to their allegedly humane principles. Such principles are marvelously flexible, however, as seen from the fact that many of the most ardent opponents of the death penalty are equally zealous in support of "abortion rights." They would spare the lives of convicted murderers, but not the lives of innocent pre-born babies. Their consciences forbid them from opposing a woman's "right to choose," even if it has cost an estimated 55 million lives since the U.S. Supreme Court's 1973 *Roe v. Wade* ruling prohibiting states from protecting prenatal life. Ours has been an age peculiar for the passage of laws to protect human health and the repeal of laws to defend human life. And yet we have consolation with us: At least those aborted in the womb have been spared the dangers of second-hand smoke.

What more should we expect from the purveyors of "progressive" thought in what T.S. Eliot described as "an age which advances progressively backwards?"

Why Christians Should Support the Death Penalty

R. Albert Mohler Jr.

R. Albert Mohler Jr. is president of the Southern Baptist Theological Seminary.

The death penalty has been part of human society for millennia, understood to be the ultimate punishment for the most serious crimes.

But, should Christians support the death penalty now, especially in light of the controversial execution Tuesday [April 29, 2014] in Oklahoma?

This is not an easy yes or no question.

The Bible's Teaching on the Death Penalty

On the one hand, the Bible clearly calls for capital punishment in the case of intentional murder.

In Genesis 9:6, God told Noah that the penalty for intentional murder should be death: "Whoever sheds the blood of man, by man shall his blood be shed, for God made man in his own image."

The death penalty was explicitly grounded in the fact that God made every individual human being in his own image, and thus an act of intentional murder is an assault upon human dignity and the very image of God.

In the simplest form, the Bible condemns murder and calls for the death of the murderer. The one who intentionally takes life by murder forfeits the right to his own life.

In the New Testament, the Apostle Paul instructs Christians that the government "does not bear the sword in vain."

Indeed, in this case the magistrate "is the servant of God, an avenger who carries out God's wrath on the evildoer" [Romans 13:4].

On the other hand, the Bible raises a very high requirement for evidence in a case of capital murder.

The act of murder must be confirmed and corroborated by the eyewitness testimony of accusers, and the society is to take every reasonable precaution to ensure that no one is punished unjustly.

While the death penalty is allowed and even mandated in some cases, the Bible also reveals that not all who are guilty of murder and complicity in murder are executed.

Just remember the biblical accounts concerning Moses, David and Saul, later known as Paul.

Christian thinking about the death penalty must begin with the fact that the Bible envisions a society in which capital punishment for murder is sometimes necessary, but should be exceedingly rare.

The Bible also affirms that the death penalty, rightly and justly applied, will have a powerful deterrent effect.

We have lost the cultural ability to declare murder—even mass murder—to be deserving of the death penalty.

In a world of violence, the death penalty is understood as a necessary firewall against the spread of further deadly violence.

Seen in this light, the problem we face today is not with the death penalty, but with society at large.

American society is quickly conforming to a secular worldview, and the clear sense of right and wrong that was Christianity's gift to Western civilization is being replaced with a much more ambiguous morality.

We have lost the cultural ability to declare murder—even mass murder—to be deserving of the death penalty.

The Problems with the Death Penalty

We have also robbed the death penalty of its deterrent power by allowing death penalty cases to languish for years in the legal system, often based on irrational and irrelevant appeals.

While most Americans claim to believe that the death penalty should be supported, there is a wide disparity in how Americans of different states and regions think about the issue.

Furthermore, Christians should be outraged at the economic and racial injustice in how the death penalty is applied. While the law itself is not prejudiced, the application of the death penalty often is.

There is very little chance that a wealthy white murderer will ever be executed. There is a far greater likelihood that a poor African-American murderer will face execution.

Why? Because the rich can afford massively expensive legal defense teams that can exhaust the ability of the prosecution to get a death penalty sentence.

This is an outrage, and no Christian can support such a disparity. As the Bible warns, the rich must not be able to buy justice on their own terms.

There is also the larger cultural context. We must recognize that our cultural loss of confidence in human dignity and the secularizing of human identity has made murder a less heinous crime in the minds of many Americans.

Most would not admit this lower moral evaluation of murder, but our legal system is evidence that this is certainly true.

Opposition to the Death Penalty

We also face a frontal assault upon the death penalty that is driven by legal activists and others determined to bring legal execution to an end in America.

Controversy over an execution this week in Oklahoma will bring even more attention to this cause, but most Americans will be completely unaware that this tragedy was caused by the inability of prison authorities to gain access to drugs for lethal injection that would have prevented those complications.

Opponents of the death penalty have, by their legal and political action, accomplished what might seem at first to be impossible—they now demand action to correct a situation that they largely created.

I believe that Christians should hope, pray and strive for a society in which the death penalty, rightly and rarely applied, would make moral sense.

Their intention is to make the death penalty so horrifying in the public mind that support for executions would disappear. They have attacked every form of execution as "cruel and unusual punishment," even though the Constitution itself authorizes the death penalty.

It is a testament to moral insanity that they have successfully diverted attention from a murderer's heinous crimes and instead put the death penalty on trial.

Christian Support for the Death Penalty

Should Christians support the death penalty today?

I believe that Christians should hope, pray and strive for a society in which the death penalty, rightly and rarely applied, would make moral sense.

This would be a society in which there is every protection for the rights of the accused, and every assurance that the social status of the murderer will not determine the sentence for the crime.

Christians should work to ensure that there can be no reasonable doubt that the accused is indeed guilty of the crime. We must pray for a society in which the motive behind capital punishment is justice, and not merely revenge.

We must work for a society that will honor every single human being at every point of development and of every race and ethnicity as made in God's image.

We must hope for a society that will support and demand the execution of justice in order to protect the very existence of that society. We must pray for a society that rightly tempers justice with mercy.

Should Christians support the death penalty today? I believe that we must, but with the considerations detailed above.

At the same time, given the secularization of our culture and the moral confusion that this has brought, this issue is not so clear-cut as some might think.

I do believe that the death penalty, though supported by the majority of Americans, may not long survive in this cultural context.

It is one thing to support the death penalty. It is another thing altogether to explain it, fix it, administer it and sustain it with justice.

We are about to find out if Americans have the determination to meet that challenge. Christians should take leadership to help our fellow citizens understand what is at stake.

God affirmed the death penalty for murder as he made his affirmation of human dignity clear to Noah. Our job is to make it clear to our neighbors.

The US Death Penalty Violates Human Rights

David A. Love

David A. Love is the executive director of Witness to Innocence, a national organization of exonerated former death row prisoners and their families.

There's a buzz about the death penalty in America these days. And nearly all of the conversation focuses not on how to maintain the practice, but rather on abolition.

The Death Penalty in the States

Connecticut just decided [2012] to repeal the death penalty, following the lead of Illinois, New Mexico and New Jersey in recent years. Meanwhile, California voters will vote on a ballot measure that would eliminate one-quarter of the nation's death row.

Faced with the high cost, lack of deterrent effect and the inevitability of executing innocent people, some states are taking another look. Moreover, given the appalling specter of prosecutors striking black jurors and other forms of racial misconduct, North Carolina and Kentucky have enacted racial justice legislation to overturn racially biased death sentences.

With the European Union enacting an export ban on lethal injection chemicals to the U.S., states are scrambling to find out how to kill people. With diminished supplies, states are faced with the option of suspending executions altogether, or like a violence addict, purchasing the poisons on the black market. In other cases such as Ohio, they have abandoned the commonly-used, three-drug protocol in favor of a single drug such as pentobarbital—a more commonly found substance used to euthanize animals.

And so, as people are still put down like dogs in the land of the free—despite the momentum for abolition—capital punishment represents America's human rights blind spot. But really, this is about more than executions. Rather, it speaks to a nation that often pays lip service to upholding human rights, but debases and denigrates human life through its actions. The result is a callous culture of violence, neglect and disregard.

One Among Many Violations

The U.S. ranked fifth in the world in capital punishment last year, in league with China, Saudi Arabia, Iran and Iraq. A world leader in executions, America is the world's foremost leader in prisons. The U.S. claims one-twentieth of the global population, but one-quarter of the world's prisoners. A majority of these prisoners are poor and of color, poorly educated, poorly represented in the courtroom and failed by the system. The warehousing of people is big business, an unseemly union of criminal justice policy and profit motive.

The death penalty is the tip of the iceberg when it comes to human rights violations in the U.S.

Is it an accident that the world's prison leader also ranks near the bottom in income inequality, boasts the largest income inequality in the developed world? Hardly not. Inequality in the land of opportunity is far more than in Europe, Canada, Australia and South Korea, but also more than nearly all of Asia, West Africa and North Africa. The top 1 percent of Americans enjoy far more than elsewhere in the West in terms of executive pay and policies favoring the rich. This, as

America's 99 percent receive far less government support for health insurance, daycare, pensions and education.

Meanwhile, as the U.S. preaches democracy to the rest of the world, it enacts voter ID laws that could potentially disenfranchise millions of citizens. Harder to vote, yet easier to purchase a gun. Leading the industrialized nations in handgun proliferation and firearms deaths, America is truly what Martin Luther King called "the greatest purveyor of violence in the world today." Lax gun laws, "shoot to kill" legislation and laws allowing concealed weapons in schools, churches, sports arenas and bars reflect the power of corporate arms manufacturers in U.S. politics. Made in America, the violence is exported to Mexico in the form of illegal weapons fueling the drug war carnage.

And this culture of violence extends to the death penalty, in a country conditioned by years of dehumanization, normalized through slavery and Jim Crow lynching. The death penalty is the tip of the iceberg when it comes to human rights violations in the U.S. It might be the most disturbing example of the human rights challenges facing the nation, and the challenges are many.

Against Capital Punishment

Charles C.W. Cooke

Charles C.W. Cooke writes for the National Review.

Let's Choose Not to Kill When We Don't Have To

Since the state of Oklahoma "botched" its execution of Clayton Lockett last week, the media have turned their fleeting attentions to the death penalty—mostly in a tone of voice that can best be described as censorious. This website, in turn, has pushed back against the impulse, Dennis Prager asking rhetorically whether "the side that can't muster outrage over murder victims" is "really the one with a heart," John Lott Jr. doing an admirable job questioning some of the sloppy thinking on the abolitionists' side, and Jonah Goldberg taking to heart Radley Balko's wise assessment that "both sides of the death-penalty debate have irreconcilable moral convictions" and concluding, for his part, that "Lockett deserved to die for what he did." "Everything else," Goldberg wrote, having run through the objections, "amounts to changing the subject, and it won't convince me otherwise."

National Review being a magazine that features a variety of different views, I thought it was about time that someone made the opposite case. So, here it is: I dissent.

While I am in agreement with their goals, I should say that many of the cases that capital punishment's opponents level against the institution strike me as being embarrassingly weak. The fashionable claim that the Eighth Amendment outlaws the practice as "cruel and unusual punishment" is not merely historically and legally illiterate—the worst of the living constitutionalists' political opportunism—but a transparent and counter-productive attempt to take away from the people a question that is ultimately theirs to decide. Also unconvincing: the breathless suggestions that a particular form of execution's causing us problems renders the whole kit and caboodle unjust (why not find a better way of carrying out the death penalty?); a popular meme that puts the United States on a similar moral plane as other users of the death penalty such as Iran, China, and North Korea—it matters, after all, for what and how you are sentencing people to death; and the insinuation that the system is inherently "racist"— which, in our era at least, appears to be highly questionable.

Better, but not perfect, is the proposition that the state's fallibility and death's finality make dangerous bedfellows. This is indisputably true. But even this line is ultimately limited in its usefulness, implying as it does that if we had perfect information, equitable sentencing, and a reliable means of offing the unwanted, then killing the guilty would be acceptable. In my view, it would not, and this, I think, is the point that should be most forcefully made. Rather than waste their time with baubles, advocates would do much better to subjugate their ancillary arguments to their essential objection: That we shouldn't be choosing to execute anybody when we don't have to.

By and large, we execute people in the United States by choice *and not by necessity.*

To my mind, this question is primarily an ethical one: Namely, "When is it acceptable to kill?" As a general rule, the best answer to this seems to be "sometimes." Mohandas Gandhi was an admirable man in many ways, but his pacifism took on a self-destructive bent that I would not recommend Americans emulate, culminating in the suggestion that the Jews of Nazi Germany should respond to the unimaginable violence that was perpetrated against them by committing mass suicide. The unfortunate truth is that, in a whole host of situations, we really do have little choice but to kill. If soldiers come over the border, guns blazing in our direction, what can we do but to fire back? When a woman is confronted by a rapist who is immune to reason and unwilling to respond to her refusals, she has little choice but to fight—to the death if needs be. If one's home is invaded and the lives of one's family members are threatened, deadly force is a wholly appropriate—and arguably mandatory—response. Life is precious. But, by its very nature, holistic pacifism has a poor answer to the question of *which* life is more precious, and when they are pitted against one another, pacifists tend to choose the lives of the aggressors while non-pacifists tend to choose the lives of the targeted.

Still, in making the case for self-defense, one needs to tease out some crucial distinctions. If a man breaks into my house and threatens me and my family, I have every right to shoot him dead. But it seems reasonable to presume that this right lasts only *for as long as he remains a threat*. What if I neutralize the threat without having to use deadly force? What if I point a gun at an attacker and he drops to the floor shouting, "Don't shoot"? What if I keep the gun trained on him and then call the police? What if I bind his hands behind his back and then involve the authorities? Would it still be acceptable for me to execute him for having put me in peril? I think not.

This situation is analogous to the death penalty in an important way. Nobody would deny that a police officer or regular citizen should be able to defend himself in the line of duty. Nevertheless, once he is safe we would all expect him to try to keep his suspect alive. Why? Well, partly because we value due process: It is, after all, not the officer's responsibility to sentence the accused to death, but his obligation to submit him to his peers for judgment. But, I'd venture, we also expect him to spare his charge because we draw a moral distinction between people who are threatening us and people who are not. Morally, does this calculation really change if the guilty person has been through a court?

The analogy is not perfect. But, by and large, we execute people in the United States by *choice* and not by necessity: as retribution, or as an example to others (which we call "deterrence"), or because it brings closure to the bereaved. We do it not so that those inside the prison gates might be safer, but so that those outside feel that justice has been served—performing in ceremony what Albert Camus called "the most premeditated of murders." Those we kill may be hideous, and their behavior may have been unspeakable. But we are appalled by them because their actions contrast so sharply with what we believe we are capable of, prompting us to share glances and to whisper in shock: "In a million years on earth, we wouldn't do anything like that."

Let's not.

CHAPTER 2

Does the Death Penalty Serve the Public Good?

Overview: The Cost of the Death Penalty

Richard Williams

*Richard Williams is a policy specialist at the National Confer-
ence of State Legislatures.*

The question of whether capital punishment is an acceptable way to administer justice has long perplexed the
nation's lawmakers and divided its citizens.

Traditional arguments pit those who believe the death
penalty has no place in a civilized society against supporters
who see it as an appropriate deterrent and punishment for the
most heinous crimes.

Capital punishment's unstable history demonstrates how
contentious the debate has been. In 1972, the U.S. Supreme
Court suspended the death penalty on the grounds it violated
the Eighth Amendment's prohibition against cruel and unusual punishment. The decision voided existing statutes in 40
states. Then in 1976, the court reauthorized capital punishment, enabling states to reenact their death penalty statutes.
Thirty-seven did, but three of those—Illinois, New Jersey and
New Mexico—have abolished their laws since 2007. With those
changes, 16 states currently do not use capital punishment.

A Costly Conviction

Although the debate continues to be rooted in philosophical
arguments, the recent legislative action abolishing the death
penalty has been spurred by practical concerns.

Richard Williams, "The Cost of Punishment," *State Legislatures*, vol. 37 no. 7, July–
August 2011, pp. 55–56. Copyright © 2011 by The National Conference of State Legislatures. All rights reserved. Reproduced by permission.

New Jersey abolished its death penalty in 2007 in large part because the state had spent $254 million over 21 years administering it without executing a single person.

"It makes more sense fiscally to have inmates be sentenced to life imprisonment without parole than to have them sit on death row and to go through the appeals process," says Senator Christopher "Kip" Bateman, the bill's sponsor. "New Jersey is going through tough times financially and any decision that is ethical in nature and promotes fiscal responsibility is a win-win for the state."

New Mexico lawmakers followed in 2009, ending capital punishment over similar cost concerns.

Many state-initiated analyses . . . have found administering capital punishment is significantly more expensive than housing prisoners for life without parole.

"There is no more inefficient law on the books than the death penalty," says Representative Antonio "Moe" Maestas, co-sponsor of the bill to repeal it. "It sounds very callous and shallow to talk about cost, but we spend other people's money, and we have to consider scarce resources."

Maestas believes his perspective is particularly persuasive because it's rooted in pragmatism rather than personal idealism. "The bottom line is, I don't care if the most heinous criminals die. They should. But capital punishment is very expensive for our state, and we have to find the best use of taxpayer dollars and prosecutorial resources. How many other murders and violent crimes cases could be prosecuted with the resources from one death penalty case?"

A Punishment Worth Preserving

Many state-initiated analyses—including reports from Michigan, New Mexico and South Dakota—have found administering capital punishment is significantly more expensive than housing prisoners for life without parole.

A study released last month [June 2011] found California has spent more than $4 billion on capital punishment since 1978, executing 13 criminals. That's about $184 million more a year than life sentences would have cost.

Much of the cost results from litigating numerous appeals during the convict's time on death row, where the average inmate spends 13 years prior to execution.

This lengthy process also influenced Bateman's decision to sponsor an abolishment bill. "I spoke to many families who went through trying emotional times during the appeals for death row inmates," he says. "Transferring an inmate from death row to life without parole allows for the aggrieved families to have a sense of calmness in their life without having to relive the tragic events over and over again."

Many believe, however, the punishment is worth preserving even though it is expensive, if it can be made more manageable.

Illinois suspended capital punishment for 11 years before abolishing it in March 2011. When former Governor George Ryan instituted the moratorium, his intent was to give Illinois time to study and improve its capital punishment procedures.

Without the death penalty ... there is no adequate punishment for the most vicious criminals.

During the moratorium, the Illinois Capital Punishment Commission and Reform Study Committee made several recommendations for improvement, including requiring the state Supreme Court to review all death sentences, setting minimum standards for DNA evidence, and increasing funding for indigent defense. The committee also recommended a full cost analysis, but it was never conducted.

The moratorium was not lifted and many, including Representative Jim Durkin, believe the reforms were not given an adequate chance. "This was not about frustration over a system that could not be made workable," he says. "This is strictly about abolitionists being morally opposed to the death penalty. That's fine, but be honest about it."

Without the death penalty, Durkin believes, there is no adequate punishment for the most vicious criminals. "A lot of these other arguments will not matter when someone is faced with the murder of a loved one."

One Crime Changes Minds

In Connecticut, the state's capital punishment abolishment debate took place at the same time as the trials for one of the most horrific crimes in the state's history, a home invasion that resulted in the murder of three members of the Petit family.

One of the killers, Steven Hayes, was convicted and sentenced to death earlier this year. Joshua Komisarjevsky, his accused accomplice, is set to go on trial in September. Many fear that making any change to Connecticut's current death penalty will make it unavailable to punish these men.

"If there were ever a case to merit the death penalty, this would be it," says Senator John Kissel. "And if the bill passed, while not retroactive, it could give these men grounds for appeal."

During the General Assembly's 2011 capital penalty debate, the Office of Fiscal Analysis reported Connecticut spends $3.3 million a year on death row cases and has performed only one execution since reinstating capital punishment in 1977. Lawmakers also heard from James Tillman, who spent 16 years in prison before DNA testing exonerated him. Some worry similar tests may one day prove the state has performed wrongful executions.

"A government that cannot guarantee the absolute accuracy of its proceedings should not take to itself the power of taking a human life," said Senator Martin Looney, referring to the Tillman case.

"Once someone is killed they are dead forever," says Senator Edith Prague, a long-time supporter of the death penalty. "Between the cost of capital punishment and the recent exonerations of innocent people, I have decided to generally support repeal."

But Prague ultimately changed her mind and cast the deciding vote against repeal after meeting with Dr. William Petit, the sole survivor of the Connecticut home invasion that robbed him of his family.

"If repeal comes up in the future, I will support it," she says. "The difference with this case is that these are the guys who did it. Their identity is not in doubt, and after meeting with Dr. Petit I know this is the right thing to do."

A Legislative See-Saw

With passionate proponents on each side, the death penalty will likely be on a repeal/reinstate see-saw indefinitely. This year, lawmakers in New Jersey and New Mexico have debated legislation to once again reinstate capital punishment. Although it's unlikely either bill will pass in 2011, the issue will be raised again in the future.

"There are certain heinous crimes that rise to the level of warranting the death penalty—killing a child, murdering a police officer, acts of terrorism," says Senator Robert Singer, the bill's sponsor in New Jersey. "Our old law had problems, but problems that can be fixed."

The Death Penalty Is an Effective Punishment

Derek Hunter

Derek Hunter is a Washington, DC-based writer, radio host, and political strategist who contributes frequently to the online magazine Townhall.

This week [August 18–24, 2013] has pissed me off. It's been a week filled with news I'd rather forget, but really, it's one we all should remember. It should be a rallying cry, an opportunity for those interested in justice to reform a broken system and expedite a punishment reserved for a deserving few.

A Horrific Murder

A college baseball player from Australia was murdered in Duncan, Okla., because three monsters were bored. The sheer convergence of bad parenting required to bring these three together and have none of them, not one, object to the idea of murdering a random stranger for lack of anything to do is as criminal as their murderous act. Their parents should sit in court next to them, charged as accessories.

The mother of Chancey Luna, one of the accused, told an Australian TV reporter she knew her son didn't do this because he was home at the time—she saw him. A few minutes later, she said she knew in her "heart" he couldn't have done this. If I had a child accused of something so heinous and I had an iron-clad alibi like "I was with him at the time," that's all I would be saying. That's not what she's saying. She's saying he's too respectful to have done something like this. But he, like every child, "likes to fight." Sick.

Chancey wasn't born evil. He became that way either through horrible parenting or horribly neglectful parenting. Whatever the case, this woman and her counterparts who created the other two evil bipeds should sit in prison with their progeny, released only after they're put to a justifiable death. Let the parents live the rest of their miserable lives with the pain their creatures imposed on the family of Christopher Lane.

A Brutal Attack

Then we move to Spokane, Wash.

Waiting for justice to happen in death penalty cases has become an inexcusably long process for families of victims.

Delbert Belton is a hero. Well, Delbert Belton was a hero. On Wednesday night, Belton, an 88-year-old veteran of World War II, became a victim of two teenage sub-human animals who beat him to death for reasons unknown. Belton, wounded in the Battle of Okinawa, was heading to a regular pool game he played weekly with his caregiver when these wastes of human flesh attacked him. He died the next day.

As of this writing, one of these beings has been arrested, the other remains at large (hopefully to be slowly run over by a steamroller or eaten alive by small woodland creatures rather than be taken into custody). May they both be slowly fed into wood chippers one appendage at a time starting with the one between their legs.

As for why these disgusting displays of inhumanity happened, I don't care. I don't want to understand these monsters, I want to eliminate them. May they be removed from the gene pool before they have a chance to infect it with their DNA.

The Impact of Opposition

Oklahoma and Washington have the death penalty, but they aren't Texas. Waiting for justice to happen in death penalty cases has become an inexcusably long process for families of victims. From 1984 to 2006, the average number of months spent on death row has increased from 74 to 145. Waiting more than 12 years for justice to be done is, in many cases, longer than the lives of the victims these killers took to get there in the first place.

In 1981, progressive hero Mumia Abu-Jamal murdered Philadelphia police officer Daniel Faulkner during a traffic stop of Mumia's brother. He shot Officer Faulkner point-blank in the face. He was sentenced to death for this disgusting murder in 1982, but anti-justice crusaders and liberal politicians and celebrities managed to deny the Faulkner family the justice they deserved and the law demanded. In 2011, Abu-Jamal's death sentence was commuted to life in prison without the possibility of parole. He'd spent 30 years on death row when he only allowed Daniel Faulkner to live 26. Only to the most disgusting corners of the progressive mind can this be seen as "justice."

But that is what progressives call it—justice. Collecting money from co-workers, friends and family members of a murder victim to provide housing, food, cable, Internet and education to the person who took a loved one from their lives—to them, that is justice.

The death penalty needs reforming. Just as the introduction of DNA evidence has freed many innocent people from death row, it also should have decreased the wait time for execution. That would be justice. But the goal of the anti-justice progressive movement is the abolition of the death penalty, not its effective use.

An Equalizer for Justice

Whether you believe in an afterlife or not, the death penalty is the greatest equalizer for justice for society's greatest monsters.

If you believe this world is all there is, that when you die you're done, then a bad day in prison is better than not existing at all. If you believe in Hell, the worst day in prison is better than the best day in Hell.

Some people knowingly do things that forfeit their right to experience even the bad things in life. And given the existence of prison weddings and conjugal visits, the sooner we weed these creatures from the herd the better. Progressives will tell you the death penalty doesn't deter crime, and that's true. It's also irrelevant. Some people are so evil and/or stupid that they don't care that they'll be executed for their actions. But where the death penalty works, where it has a 100 percent success rate, is recidivism. No executed criminal has ever harmed another innocent human being.

We had two examples of sub-human activity that is deserving of the ultimate penalty—five people whose actions should be met with the absolute justice we can bestow. They probably won't get it. A deal will be cut, or even if they do they'll live long, unproductive lives on the public dole.

The Death Penalty Protects Society from the Most Evil Criminals

Matt K. Lewis

Matt K. Lewis is a contributing editor at TheWeek.com and a senior contributor for The Daily Caller.

On Tuesday night [April 29, 2014], Oklahoma prisoner Clayton Lockett died of a heart attack after the lethal injection cocktail that was supposed to kill him didn't work.

A Botched Execution

Pretty much everyone admits that the execution of this convicted murderer was "botched." My colleague Andrew Cohen bemoans the apparent judicial failings that led up to the failed execution. The White House declared that the whole thing fell short of "humane standards."

This is regrettable. But I won't be losing any sleep over it.

Now obviously, a speedy and painless execution would have been better than what Lockett endured. But when you shoot a 19-year-old woman, and then watch as your buddies bury her alive, you sort of forfeit the right to complain about such things.

Of course, my writing this will make me a pariah to the liberal people arguing that this monster should be treated more compassionately.

In any event, this failed execution in Oklahoma has catapulted the topic of capital punishment back into the national spotlight. So this is perhaps a good opportunity to explain why a "bleeding heart conservative" such as yours truly still supports the death penalty (if only in cases of especially heinous acts.)

Political Leanings and the Death Penalty

This isn't a clear-cut Right versus Left issue, of course. A lot of conservatives oppose capital punishment. Some social conservatives see support of the death penalty as inconsistent with opposition to abortion. (The difference, of course, is that unborn babies are innocent.)

To many liberals, it seems that it is deemed more civilized—more evolved—to care about the life of a murderer (or the Nevada desert tortoise) than that of an unborn child (or, for that matter, Lockett's 19-year-old victim). I will never understand this way of thinking, but the very words we use imply we believe it. As Erick Erickson has said, "For liberals a botched execution is when the convict dies, a botched abortion is when the innocent live."

I believe in second chances. I believe in reform and rehabilitation. But I also believe in evil.

Other small-government conservatives and libertarians argue that it is inconsistent for people who already distrust big government to grant it the power of life and death over its citizens. As a conservative who believes in *ordered* liberty, and that it is a responsibility of government to protect its citizens, this argument doesn't dissuade me—especially now that DNA testing can and should be used to exonerate the wrongly accused.

Declining crime rates have also given a new crop of conservative reformers the luxury of re-evaluating the "tough on crime" policies that were birthed out of necessity amid the crime and lawlessness of the 1970s, when it seemed the center could not hold. This was around the time when Irving Kristol described a neoconservative as "a liberal mugged by reality." My guess is that the declining crime rate helps explain why a "shrinking majority of Americans" favor the death penalty today. This seems to be a new trend. The death penalty was once so popular—and the "soft on crime" tag so damaging—that presidential candidate Bill Clinton refused to grant clemency to a mentally impaired man named Rickey Ray Rector. This case is reminiscent of the Lockett incident, in that, as the *AP* reported, "The execution was delayed by nearly an hour because medical personnel were not able to find a suitable vein in which to inject the solution."

Now, count me among those who believe mandatory minimum sentences for minor drug crimes ought to be reconsidered—and who think it's a mistake to take somebody who is guilty of possession of a small amount of marijuana and put them in a cage with violent criminals. (Pat Nolan of Prison Fellowship probably put it best when he said. "We have prisons for people we're afraid of, but we've been filling them with folks we're just mad at.")

I believe in second chances. I believe in reform and rehabilitation. But I also believe in evil.

While capital punishment may not be a deterrent (the infrequency of its use almost guarantees this), the recidivism rate is astonishingly low.

The Proper Use of the Death Penalty

Twisted rapists and murderers are not in the same universe of criminal as drug users and thieves. So even as we slash mandatory minimum sentences and reform our prison system, I do not believe we should abandon capital punishment for most extreme cases.

You really can't take someone like Clayton Lockett and reform him—or, at least, the odds of doing so are unfathomable. This wasn't a crime of passion. He didn't walk into his house, see his wife in bed with another man, fly into a rage, kill him, and then immediately feel remorse. He shot a 19-year-old woman and then watched his friends bury her alive. Try to reform that.

So what can you do? You *certainly* can't put him back on the street. You could give him life in prison and a PlayStation 3. But as the son of a prison guard from Maryland, let me assure you: Inmates who have no hope of earning an early release also have no incentive not to harm or kill correctional officers or other inmates. And solitary confinement is arguably a crueler and more unusual form of punishment than the death penalty.

And there's also this: While capital punishment may not be a deterrent (the infrequency of its use almost guarantees this), the recidivism rate is astonishingly low. I mean, there are very few repeat offenders.

So yes, we ought to make sure we get to the bottom of what went wrong with this lethal injection. But no, we shouldn't do too much hand-wringing and pearl-clutching along the way. At the end of the day, the death penalty should be safe, legal, rare—and utterly efficient.

The Death Penalty Is a Deterrent to Murder

William Tucker

William Tucker is a journalist and author of Vigilante: The Backlash Against Crime in America.

There's a concept in economics I think ought to be introduced into the public discourse. It's called the "marginal value of wealth." It means that the wealthier you become, the less each additional dollar means to you. That's why we have environmentalism—because some people have grown so affluent that they really aren't much interested in further economic development.

The Purpose of the Death Penalty

The same concept also applies to crime. There's a "marginal value of safety" that people take into account when evaluating policies such as the death penalty. Most affluent Americans now feel safe enough in their suburban retreats or gated communities with private police patrols so that they can express more concern for a condemned criminal suffering a few minutes of pain in a botched execution than for what the person did to end up on death row in the first place. (As many have pointed out, all this blundering could be fast eliminated by returning to the firing squad.)

It's a different story, however, if you're running a bodega in a low-income neighborhood or working in a 7-Eleven on a lonely Texas highway. You are completely vulnerable. You may be protected by security cameras or a locked cash register, but to an amateur with a handgun this means little. Murder is the third cause of occupational death among men, behind vehicle accidents and falls by construction workers, and the leading cause of occupational death among women. There's a very simple reason. For a criminal pulling off a holdup—or a rapist, or a "surprised" burglar caught by a homeowner—there's a very simple logic at work. The victims of your crimes are also the principal witnesses. They will call the police the minute you depart. They can identify you. They will probably testify at your trial. There's a very simple way to prevent all this: kill them.

After the death penalty was abolished, murder rates nearly tripled, rising to an all-time high in the 1980s.

The purpose of the death penalty is to draw a bright line between a felony and felony murder. If the penalty for rape or robbery is jail time, and for murder is more jail time after that, there isn't a huge incentive to prevent you from pulling the trigger. This was well known to reformers of the eighteenth century, who tried to resolve the same dilemma by eliminating the death penalty for crimes less than homicide. In *The Spirit of the Laws* (1750), Montesquieu wrote:

> It is a great abuse among us to condemn to the same punishment a person what only robs on the highway and another who robs and murders. Surely, for the public security, some difference should be made in the punishment.

> In China, those who add murder to robbery are cut in pieces: but not so the others; to this difference it is owing that though they rob in that country they never murder.

> In Russia, where the punishment of robbery and murder is the same, they always murder. The dead, they say, tell no tales.

bers and friends of Hernandez also confessed that he had killed Lopez. In my view, the execution of even one innocent person is too many.

The Death Penalty Does Not Deter Crime

The available evidence indicates that the death penalty does not reduce murder rates. FBI Unified Crime reports show that states with the death penalty have homicide rates 48–101% *higher* than states without the death penalty. Similarly, an international study of criminal violence analyzed data from 110 nations over a period of 74 years and found that the death penalty does not deter criminals. One reason why the death penalty might not deter criminals is that most murders are committed in a fit of rage, after an intense argument, when people rarely consider the consequences of their actions. Former U.S. Attorney General Janet Reno said: "I have inquired for most of my adult life about studies that might show that the death penalty is a deterrent. And I have not seen any research that would substantiate that point."

The U.S. is one of the few countries in the world that has executed minors under 18-years-old.

The Death Penalty Targets the Poor

Of the 22,000 murders that occur each year in the U.S., about 1% result in death sentences. Which 1% depends largely on the effectiveness of the attorney, which often depends on how much money the accused has. U.S. Supreme Court Justice Ruth Bader Ginsburg said, "People who are well represented at trial do not get the death penalty." Ginsburg also criticized the "meager" amount of money spent to defend poor people. OJ Simpson's lawyer—who received $5 million for defending him—said, "In the U.S., you're better off, if you're in the system being guilty and rich than being innocent and poor." There are no billionaires or millionaires on death row.

The Deterrent Effect

In the 1960s we stopped executing people altogether. At the time homicides were at an historical low and 90 percent were "acquaintance" murders resulting from disputes between friends or relatives. "Stranger murders," which are generally committed in the course of other crimes, had been reduced to 10 percent. What happened next is well-established. After the death penalty was abolished, murder rates nearly tripled, rising to an all-time high in the 1980s. Only when the death penalty was reinstated and states started executing people in significant numbers in the 1990s did they again fall to 1960s levels. The 500,000 murders committed during this interim took more lives than any conflict in American history save the Civil War. Moreover, by the 1980s murder in the act of another crime had risen to about half the much larger total.

But of course these murders were not evenly distributed across society. Instead they are still highly concentrated in minority neighborhoods. Although African Americans make up only 13 percent of the population, they constitute 48 percent of all murder victims—93 percent of whom are killed by other blacks—and they commit 51 percent of the murders in which the case is solved. A standard argument against the death penalty is that it is racist because 40 percent of those on death row are African American. But in fact judges and juries are six times less likely to impose capital punishment if the victim is black. There is racism in the system, but it is not the kind people think.

The late Ernest van den Haag used to suggest that we should only execute people for murders on odd numbered days, just to see whether criminals would shift their activities. In fact, we have been conducting just such an experiment by race for decades. What better proof could we have that the death penalty makes a difference?

The Death Penalty Is a Flawed Form of Punishment

Brad Bushman

Brad Bushman is a professor of communication and psychology at Ohio State University.

In Old Testament times, the death penalty was used as the punishment for murder. But death was also the punishment for a number of other offenses, such as eating leavened bread during the Feast of Unleavened Bread, being a stubborn child, picking up sticks on the Sabbath day, insulting your parents, going to the Tabernacle if you are not a priest, and ignoring the verdict of a judge or priest. Today the death penalty is still used in 32 states in America, including the state I live in—Ohio.

Seven Problems with the Death Penalty

In 2007 the American Bar Association released the results of a three-year study of the death penalty. Although the American Bar Association takes no position for or against the death penalty, they issued a moratorium on the death penalty because "the process is deeply flawed." As a researcher of aggression and violence for over 25 years, I also believe the death penalty is "deeply flawed." There are at least seven serious problems with the death penalty.

The Death Penalty Models the Behavior it Seeks to Prevent

The death penalty is used to deter killers, but it models the very behavior it seeks to prevent. It teaches the lesson that it is acceptable to kill, as long as the state is the one doing the killing. Hence the term "capital punishment." This is somewhat paradoxical. As my friend Jed said, "We don't like people who kill other people, so to show everyone how much we don't like people who kill people, we are going to kill people who kill other people. It seems like capital punishment pretty much goes against everything it claims to be for." The death penalty answers violence with counter-violence. As American novelist Wendell Berry said, "Violence breeds violence. Acts of violence committed in 'justice' or in affirmation of 'rights' or in defense of 'peace' do not end violence. They prepare and justify its continuation."

The available evidence indicates that the death penalty does not reduce murder rates.

You Might Kill the Wrong Person!

William Blackstone, the English jurist, judge, and Tory politician of the 18th century, said, "Better that ten guilty persons escape than that one innocent suffer." The death penalty is irreversible, so it is critical that it be used on the actual killer. Over 140 people have been exonerated and freed from death row, such as on the basis of DNA evidence. Since the U.S. Supreme Court reinstated the death penalty in 1976, 1,362 individuals have been executed in the U.S. (as of January 16, 2014). It is difficult to know for sure how many innocent people have been executed, but it appears at least 10 have. For example, Carlos DeLuna was executed in 1989 for the 1983 murder of Wanda Lopez in Corpus Christi, Texas. The only eyewitness to the crime identified DeLuna while he was sitting in the back of a police car parked in a dimly lit lot in front of the crime scene. There was no blood, DNA evidence, or fingerprints linking DeLuna to the crime. The actual murderer was a man named Carlos Hernandez, a violent criminal who [was] very similar in appearance [to] DeLuna. Hernandez even bragged about how he had murdered Lopez and gotten someone else to take the fall for him. Family mem-

The Deterrent Effect

In the 1960s we stopped executing people altogether. At the time homicides were at an historical low and 90 percent were "acquaintance" murders resulting from disputes between friends or relatives. "Stranger murders," which are generally committed in the course of other crimes, had been reduced to 10 percent. What happened next is well-established. After the death penalty was abolished, murder rates nearly tripled, rising to an all-time high in the 1980s. Only when the death penalty was reinstated and states started executing people in significant numbers in the 1990s did they again fall to 1960s levels. The 500,000 murders committed during this interim took more lives than any conflict in American history save the Civil War. Moreover, by the 1980s murder in the act of another crime had risen to about half the much larger total.

But of course these murders were not evenly distributed across society. Instead they are still highly concentrated in minority neighborhoods. Although African Americans make up only 13 percent of the population, they constitute 48 percent of all murder victims—93 percent of whom are killed by other blacks—and they commit 51 percent of the murders in which the case is solved. A standard argument against the death penalty is that it is racist because 40 percent of those on death row are African American. But in fact judges and juries are six times less likely to impose capital punishment if the victim is black. There is racism in the system, but it is not the kind people think.

The late Ernest van den Haag used to suggest that we should only execute people for murders on odd numbered days, just to see whether criminals would shift their activities. In fact, we have been conducting just such an experiment by race for decades. What better proof could we have that the death penalty makes a difference?

The Death Penalty Is a Flawed Form of Punishment

Brad Bushman

Brad Bushman is a professor of communication and psychology at Ohio State University.

In Old Testament times, the death penalty was used as the punishment for murder. But death was also the punishment for a number of other offenses, such as eating leavened bread during the Feast of Unleavened Bread, being a stubborn child, picking up sticks on the Sabbath day, insulting your parents, going to the Tabernacle if you are not a priest, and ignoring the verdict of a judge or priest. Today the death penalty is still used in 32 states in America, including the state I live in—Ohio.

Seven Problems with the Death Penalty

In 2007 the American Bar Association released the results of a three-year study of the death penalty. Although the American Bar Association takes no position for or against the death penalty, they issued a moratorium on the death penalty because "the process is deeply flawed." As a researcher of aggression and violence for over 25 years, I also believe the death penalty is "deeply flawed." There are at least seven serious problems with the death penalty.

The Death Penalty Models the Behavior it Seeks to Prevent

The death penalty is used to deter killers, but it models the very behavior it seeks to prevent. It teaches the lesson that it is acceptable to kill, as long as the state is the one doing the killing. Hence the term "capital punishment." This is somewhat paradoxical. As my friend Jed said, "We don't like people who kill other people, so to show everyone how much we don't like people who kill people, we are going to kill people who kill other people. It seems like capital punishment pretty much goes against everything it claims to be for." The death penalty answers violence with counter-violence. As American novelist Wendell Berry said, "Violence breeds violence. Acts of violence committed in 'justice' or in affirmation of 'rights' or in defense of 'peace' do not end violence. They prepare and justify its continuation."

The available evidence indicates that the death penalty does not reduce murder rates.

You Might Kill the Wrong Person!

William Blackstone, the English jurist, judge, and Tory politician of the 18th century, said, "Better that ten guilty persons escape than that one innocent suffer." The death penalty is irreversible, so it is critical that it be used on the actual killer. Over 140 people have been exonerated and freed from death row, such as on the basis of DNA evidence. Since the U.S. Supreme Court reinstated the death penalty in 1976, 1,362 individuals have been executed in the U.S. (as of January 16, 2014). It is difficult to know for sure how many innocent people have been executed, but it appears at least 10 have. For example, Carlos DeLuna was executed in 1989 for the 1983 murder of Wanda Lopez in Corpus Christi, Texas. The only eyewitness to the crime identified DeLuna while he was sitting in the back of a police car parked in a dimly lit lot in front of the crime scene. There was no blood, DNA evidence, or fingerprints linking DeLuna to the crime. The actual murderer was a man named Carlos Hernandez, a violent criminal who [was] very similar in appearance [to] DeLuna. Hernandez even bragged about how he had murdered Lopez and gotten someone else to take the fall for him. Family members and friends of Hernandez also confessed that he had killed Lopez. In my view, the execution of even one innocent person is too many.

The Death Penalty Does Not Deter Crime

The available evidence indicates that the death penalty does not reduce murder rates. FBI Unified Crime reports show that states with the death penalty have homicide rates 48–101% *higher* than states without the death penalty. Similarly, an international study of criminal violence analyzed data from 110 nations over a period of 74 years and found that the death penalty does not deter criminals. One reason why the death penalty might not deter criminals is that most murders are committed in a fit of rage, after an intense argument, when people rarely consider the consequences of their actions. Former U.S. Attorney General Janet Reno said: "I have inquired for most of my adult life about studies that might show that the death penalty is a deterrent. And I have not seen any research that would substantiate that point."

The U.S. is one of the few countries in the world that has executed minors under 18-years-old.

The Death Penalty Targets the Poor

Of the 22,000 murders that occur each year in the U.S., about 1% result in death sentences. Which 1% depends largely on the effectiveness of the attorney, which often depends on how much money the accused has. U.S. Supreme Court Justice Ruth Bader Ginsburg said, "People who are well represented at trial do not get the death penalty." Ginsburg also criticized the "meager" amount of money spent to defend poor people. OJ Simpson's lawyer—who received $5 million for defending him—said, "In the U.S., you're better off, if you're in the system being guilty and rich than being innocent and poor." There are no billionaires or millionaires on death row.